T0005919

SAYING YES

SAYING YES

DISANT OUI

2015 Black Moss Press

Library and Archives Canada Cataloguing in Publication

Saying yes / edited by Lisa Salfi & Jay Rankin.

ISBN 978-0-88753-549-9 (paperback)

1. Canadian poetry (English)--21st century. 2. Canadian
prose literature (English)--21st century. I. Rankin, Jay editor
II. Salfi, Lisa, editor

PS8251.1.S29 2015   C810.8'006   C2015-903909-6

Cover Image by Asil Moussa
Edited & Designed by Lisa Salfi & Jay Rankin

Published by Black Moss Press at 2450 Byng Road, Windsor, Ontario
N8W 3E8. Canada. Black Moss books are distributed in Canada and the
U.S. by Fitzhenry & Whiteside. All orders should be directed there.
      Fitzhenry & Whiteside
      195 Allstate Parkway
      Markham, ON
      L3R 4T8

Black Moss would like to acknowledge the generous financial support
from both the Canada Council for the Arts and the Ontario Arts Council.

ONTARIO ARTS COUNCIL
CONSEIL DES ARTS DE L'ONTARIO
an Ontario government agency
un organisme du gouvernement de l'Ontario

Canada Council Conseil des arts
for the Arts   du Canada

CONTENTS

FOREWORD

When I sit back down at the long table that faces out onto the patchwork hills spotted with white beauties and a sunset that can't be captured in a picture, I reflect on my second opportunity to experience all that La Roche d'Hys has to offer.

I start by reflecting on what I learned two years ago when I ate my first lunch and last dinner at this same table. I learned that when Marty Gervais offers you the chance to join him in Burgundy, France for a ten-day writing retreat, you say yes. You say yes because there is a long dinner table on the side of a hill that will teach you about friendship—about listening to stories of pain, silliness and love from the person on your left and on your right. You will learn about Howard and Jeanette's vision for this art farm that brings the creative community together from all over the world no matter how young or old they are. You learn that wine and cheese and bread are in fact good for you, because they feed your soul. You learn about history and culture and locals who have seen everything from the French Resistance to the French translator on an iPod. But most of all you learn that the next time you are offered an opportunity to return to this never-ending place of wisdom, you jump on a plane and go.

As I sit here on the night of the last dinner of our 2013 adventure at La Roche d'Hys, I've learned even more than I thought was possible at this long table. I learned that the sound of a live piano can fill up an entire valley with inspiration; that the art of memorization is still alive; that snail mail can withstand generations, even with the temptation of an instant message; and that Jeanette is still an amazing cook and Howard is still a terrifying driver.

This table taught me that you can never capture enough pictures of the cows; that people who claim they aren't writers can bring you to tears with their moving words; that some people are more comfortable singing their words...which can also bring you to tears; that rabbit is not chicken and moules taste best with frites; that you can be any race, religion or gender and still have a complete stranger look out for your beliefs; that no topic is safe when there is a redheaded Irish girl at the table.

I hope that when you read the following pages of poems and short stories that you feel like you are sitting at that table with us. I hope that you learn that being impulsive is a good thing and that saying yes is a life mantra. I hope that you're inspired to experience your first lunch and last dinner at that long table, even if it's in Rome, London, Windsor or Toronto, because there are always stories to be told and meals to be eaten.

Jessica Minervini

HOW TO WRITE ABOUT THIS PERFECT PLACE
Caitlyn Gray

Before you begin:

1. Smile, see, hear, explore, eat, and discover
2. Try something new
3. Don't forget: you aren't putting your words in prison—you are setting them free
4. Don't forget: it's okay to fall in love with someplace that isn't home

To write of Burgundy:

1. Fix your eyes on the swollen greenery, the White Beauties, the red currants, the roundabouts, the chardonnay and the pinot noir, the *Époisses*, and everything else you possibly can
2. Fix your eyes upon the page
3. Fix the little hole within you that your silence has created
4. Fix your mind upon this
   eternal
          burning
                 passionate

challenge

AND GOD SAID...
Gillian Cott

(For Howard and Jeannette Aster)

A very long time ago,
before God was singular,
the gods said,
"Let there be a rock and let there be a spring
where humans can come to heal.
Let this place be called La Roche d'Hys."

Then, when only one God remained,
God said,
"Let there be a church
and let there be a cross placed on a pagan rock
and let humans come from around the world to worship
only me."

Many years later,
at the same jagged rock,
now carved with stairs
up to heaven,
God said,
"Let there be madness.
Let everyone see how people can suffer
for if they yearn to love without condition
they must understand the effects of hate."
Then He said,
"Let there be people who try to end sadness
for humans' capacity for goodness is greater
than their ability for madness.
Let there be a doctor who helps heal

without a pagan spring,
but uses his hands and his heart."

However, God had already created rules
and people to make laws.
And though he gave humans the ability to hope,
it came with the opportunity for free will
to blame and to punish
to help and to heal.
Resisting madness became a war in itself.
And God knew that life was suffering so God said,
"Let the doctor die
but let his story be told.
Let it inspire the goodness in people.
Let it bloom in hearts like roses
warm from stone walls.
And when the doctor's farm is burned down,
let one room remain:
the proof of struggle,
a symbol of strength."

And through all this, God thought,
"Let there be dreams,
and let the wildest ones be the most beautiful."
And so God created two dreamers.
And they said,
"Let there be a place for musicians.
Let there be a place for singers, for writers, painters, chefs,
sommeliers, Buddhists, doctors, theoretical physicists, dancers,
teachers, and farmers.
And let this place move all of them."

So they built this dream on the doctor's farm.
They told the doctor's story
and all of the stories before.
And God said,
"This is good."

It made God smile,
and the result
was sunbeams at sunset
beside clouds that carried
the weight of centuries
but made the coucher du soleil shine brighter.
So He pulled people
from small pockets around the world
with secret stories and large laughter
with mousy voices and big hearts
to watch the sun set together.
And though they were strangers, they built friendships
and made memories.
God wanted these people to truly experience life.
So He said,
"Let there be sadness, and let there be heartbreak.
But let the magic of both the people and the place
heal you."

And one night, after God had turned too much water into wine,
He thought of everyone visiting this farm
and He said,
"Let there be feasting and seemingly unlimited wine.
Let jokes be told, and poetry be read.
Let there be tears, but let there be laughter,
and on occasion, let your laughter turn to tears."
Finally,

when He knew he was close to perfection,
God said,
"Let there be Époisses."

And then, He looked at what He had created:
twenty strangers,
lit by moonlight and tea candles
filling the length of a banquet table,
cheese on every plate,
red wine in every glass,
no conversation end in sight.
And He said,
"This is good."
So God rested.
And the musicians, singers, writers, painters, chefs, sommeliers,
Buddhists, doctors, theoretical physicists, dancers, teachers, and
farmers
kept creating.

LA ROCHE D'HYS,
Jay Rankin

We came to you, overpacked dufflebags and shoulder-tearing backpacks. We came to you, jet-lagged red eyes dropping to your soft, green grass. We came to wash our sweaty palms in your healing waters. To wash away that stink from the jetliners and cesspool of sweaty tourists swarming Paris.

And Troy did not fall this time because your gentle rolling hills and greener-than-green forests opened arms to us. And you did not laugh at us when we stood upon the rock that is you and pretended we were flying among the cross and grass and shrubs that reach for the sky upon your back. You did not laugh when I stubbed my toe and ate your dirt nor when the cows flinched from my touch.

And when someone stops by and asks me about you, I have to sit them down for an hour and I'm just done day one but there's still more to tell and my coffee's cold.

And those days when we ventured from you, I missed swinging in your hammock, napping and writing while the gentle wind carried whiffs of the spices of the province that your inhabitants love to cook with.

And people say the hands of Howard that tend you turn crazy when they grip a steering wheel. But have they seen a bus try to steamroll two cars? A bus filled with demonic children, glaring and pointing and growling. Have they seen how a car can almost clip a photographer, catching poppies on the side of the road?

When I left your earthly bosom, sandwiched between rock, forest and farm valley, I cried. We cried. And Canada flooded with our tears.

LET'S PLAY A GAME
Priscilla Bernauer

Cows play jury.
Julian Dowager plays judge.

Round 1:
What is Ashly's actual favourite animal?
What author does Caitlyn erotically recite?
What keeps Angelica and Priscilla from hearing the meal bell?

Round 2:
How many people does it take to Harlem Shake at La Roche D'Hys?
How many people does it take to drink a bottle of Rosé? (if it's just me, you only need one)
How many people does it take to let Priscilla out of the bathroom?

Round 3:
Who's a jolly good fellow?
Who is Julian Dowager?
Who poured my most recent glass of Rosé?

SMILE, YOU'RE IN FRANCE
Caitlyn Gray

Smile because you're far from home
Smile because here, you're just a pretty face in a crowd
Smile because the sun is out and the wind is cool and the day is good

No, the day is beautiful

Smile because you're you and because today, you own the city
Smile at the boy in Le Jardin du Luxembourg who's wearing blue shoes,
because he's fast asleep in the sunlight, and his hair looks so brown and soft
Smile when the girls who speak Spanish run giggling to you for pictures
Their smiles are contagious
Smile because you Said Yes

Smile because you may not find this beauty back at home
Smile because you remembered sunscreen today
And remembered the time you were here last
It was 2009 and the sky was grey
Smile because you'll be here again

Smile because there's a painter, a sweet smell in the air, statues,
fountains, and a parade of preschoolers
Smile because someone thought you were pretty
Smile because Paris isn't Burgundy, because you don't want it to be,
because they are two different kinds of lovely

Smile because you don't know where you're going
But Paris is the most wonderful walking city—a wandering city
The perfect place to lose your way
And to pick up pieces of yourself once you've found it

BURGUNDIAN RAIN
Angelica Lachance

Burgundy is filled with the richest and most innocent type of beauty I've ever seen, and it permeates everything. Rolling hills spotted with fields. Old architecture filled with cracks and vines. Freshly washed laundry blowing in the wind. Wine glasses that sparkle like new despite being used even more than cutlery. Complete and utter silence. Playing grand pianos in the loft of a barn for the first time like no one else in the world is listening.

But when you've seen enough of this world, you know better and you see beneath the surface. You see secret passageways that had to be there for a reason and the Croix de Lorraine that symbolizes French resistance to something much darker than they ever thought they'd know. But that was the 40s and this is now, and it's harder to see pain in something like that now when you can see things like beauty instead and a little mark of a big history right before your eyes.

And as darker clouds begin to cover the cotton sky you've seen in the past days, you look up and over the rolling hills wearing a look of pure confusion upon your face because you don't see how a place like this could be any more beautiful. You think that it can't, but then you find out you're wrong because just when you start to believe that, it rains. And there is something so striking about the pouring rain because of its unmatched strength and because it gives no mercy until it has finally had its say.

And this might seem wrong to you because who would take pouring rain and dark skies over the alternative of a clear, vibrant blue? But you can't really see its beauty until you're standing in the middle of it and letting it fall on every ounce you and listening to its every word and every message that lives within every drop.

And when it stops, you find yourself cursing it because you've never felt so connected to it, and you've never understood its purpose until you let it soak deep into you. Until you let the rain fall beneath your skin's surface, you never really get it. The rain shows times of trouble, but also times to start anew; rain means a kind of falling that gives no way to rescue.

DEAR TYLER (JULY 2ND, 2013)
Ashly Flannery

The first day on the farm was enough for me to know that my life would never be the same. Being in a place that gives you the chance to look within yourself and really think makes the rest of your life, for at least a couple of weeks, seem like it's full of possibility. That feeling is so overwhelming and important and impossible to hold onto forever. The only beings on the farm that I think hold onto that feeling always are the amazing White Beauties. I know I haven't mentioned them yet and I for that I'm sure I will be punished somewhere down the line. It went something like this.

On the way down the scarily winding road to the farm there were tiny white dots off in the distance and the faint smell of manure. With my advanced knowledge of farms (nothing) I deduced that the white dots must be cows. Oh wait; did I mention the cows already? Shit, well, they were cows but they were way off in the distance so they didn't really register on my radar. Anyways, as the car pulled in my attention was brought to the patchwork green fields surrounding the incredible farmhouse. Potted flowers were all in a row along the walkway into the house; I could smell them from the car. Walking through the house, the floors creaked and the walls were covered in ridiculously exaggerated wallpaper; it reminded me of what you would find in a palace back in the day. The house even smelled old. Big bedrooms filled with beds to accommodate all the people that search out solace were around every corner. Funny winding stairs that would seem impossible to fit a bag through swirled their way up to the attic studio. Huge windows built into the sides of the roof to let the light in and the inspiration flow. The view was incredible. If you didn't look carefully you would miss the tiny walkway just past the stairs that leads into the other side of the farmhouse. More beds to house more minds and down the back stairs into the SECOND kitchen—the house never seemed to end. It's a place to encourage the imagination, to find your own Narnia—if it was going to happen anywhere it was going to happen here. Out the back door, down the rock path lined with flowers and on the lawn were two long tables surrounded by chairs—meals, conversation and readings among the delicacies served out here. A little further into the outdoors and tucked away in a tiny grove of willows was a hammock, a perfect getaway for private thoughts. I never wanted to leave this place. I thought that I was as happy as I could be, that is until dinner.

We were eating a delicious beef meal. I don't remember exactly what but I remember the beef. As I finished my last bite I looked to my right and noticed that those tiny white dots from earlier were actually much closer. In fact a mere 100 metres away on the very edge of the fence separating the field from the house was a group of beautiful white cows just hanging out. I obviously abandoned my plate, grabbed my phone/camera and ran for the fence. As I approached the fence at least 10 pairs of seemingly brown eyes noticed my arrival. Deep throated mooing and slow blinking was all the reaction I got for the time being. Only after skillfully balancing myself over a nettle bush, staking my territory and making my presence known did they start to approach. I could see the muscles moving under their thick white skin as they swayed back in forth in indecision over coming to see me. The first one made her move. She took three steps towards me, stopped, blinked and moved again. I guess those first few steps were just like starting a motor because as soon as she really started moving there was no stopping her. As she made her way towards me, the rest followed, all blinking in curiosity. I took this time to introduce myself, tell them I was not there to hurt them (even though I just finished eating one of their own) and that I just wanted to take a couple of pictures of their beautiful selves. They seemed to understand me, like me even, because they made their way almost close enough to touch. I could hear my classmates laughing at how the cows reacted to me. I can hear my very own France nickname—Cow Whisperer—being shouted from the dinner table just a little ways away. I liked it!

I settled in over my nettle bush, carefully balancing on the heels of my feet, praying I wouldn't topple over, and stared into the 10 pairs of eyes staring back at me. The Beauties all took turns stomping one hoof at a time, blinking and shaking the flies from their faces. I was mesmerized. Their long eyelashes almost looked fake. I would kill for eyelashes that long. I could see them all breathing deeply, the muscles along their sides stretching in and out to accommodate each breath. I was surprised by how immensely powerful they look. I always thought cows were just big cuddly animals that we eventually eat. Not these cows. Well we do eat them but they are not just big and cuddly. As the sun set behind the hills a golden hue slid its way downwards, bouncing off the tops of the Beauties' backs, giving them a heavenly glow. My camera was no longer the only one present. My classmates were gathered at the fence, Marty was playing The Wedding March to the Beauties from behind us and I think they liked it. There was this moment of pure connection. The Beauties brought us together. We became a part of the Beauties. They are the essence of this farm and I suspect the essence of this whole trip.

This morning I wake up with this thought very fresh in my head. I can hear the Beauties just outside my window. At first it is an incredibly peaceful moment, birds, breeze and gently mooing just outside. Then as the noise picks up and I creep further into consciousness I realize that the Beauties as we so fondly call them sound like a bunch of T-Rex romping around in the field. It's a terrifying image that fully jars me into the waking world and I wonder what are we doing today?

DAILY OBSERVATIONS
Asil Moussa

Day 1: I wonder if the cows know they're one of the major highlights of our trip.

Day 2: I interviewed a really special person today. I want to tell stories for the rest of my life.

Day 3: There's an awful lot of bugs here. The bee in the sink and spider on my pillow would agree.

Day 4: People in France never waste any amount of food. They literally wipe their plates clean with their bread. It's wonderful.

Day 5: I'm still not fully convinced this spectacular view is real—waiting for the green screen to go blank.

Day 6: In the car today, Marty danced to a song called "Bubble Butt." I will remember this every time he gives a class lecture.

Day 7: Evening readings are where we go around the table sharing parts of ourselves and connect through words, laughs, and nods of understanding.

Day 8: I met the real-life Jay Gatsby today. His name is Jim Haynes. He's 80 going on 35 and endlessly fascinating.

Day 9: Howard made rabbit for dinner. I was too chicken to try it.

Day 10: I visited Shakespeare and Company today. How is it possible to feel so at home in a place you've never spent a full hour in?

Day 11: I'm really going to miss this place. And the people. And the chocolate croissants.

MOO-ABLE BEAST (JULY 1, 11:55 P.M.)
Jay Rankin

The first course is of cucumbers and tomato salad, leaves with vinegar and oil to splash on top, pickles, olives green and black, a salad with corn and something else that accompanies this veggie course, crunching between my molars.

Baskets of bread are passed around. Tear and wipe up oily drippings. The wine flows. Names I can hardly pronounce. Chardonnay? White is simple but its too *blanc*.

A shout. The white bessies have arrived. The cows graze closer and closer and closer to the fence. Horns bolt up. They see me. I reach between rusted iron bars. The herd flinches at human hands.

And they munch, crunching on their earthly grass. True vegans with horns that butt a side and side a butt.

Horns point me out as a foreigner. *"Parlez-vous Français?"* they ask.

My *"Oui"* fools none. They know I'm Canadian.

A course of meat is served, tended by the careful hands of Gillian. Rip meat off chicken bone, smother French sausage and steak with Howard's homemade dijon-esque tomato sauce. Soak up leftovers with parsley-laden rice stuff. You know, the kind of rice that isn't rice and I can never remember the name of. Wipe up juices with the baguette sponge and wash down with a glass of vin rouge.

More cows. I ran last time. My excitement carried my face into a French kiss *avec la terre*. Nice and slow—I've baked my belly and stewed my mind. My big toe feels about an inch shorter.

The bessies nudge closer when I stick my hand through rusted iron bars. A cow braves the stranger, brushes nose to human finger. He bolts back. Two other cows step forward to protect.

A barrage of shooting retaliates. They survive, their white hides stolen and digitized.

I try feeding them grass. "*Je le* swear it isn't roofied."

They don't trust me. I want to say, "*Je suis Canadien.*" And repeat until they get the picture. "It's Canada Day, you see."

Non. The cows point horns. They're a vicious gang, after all. None of the other cows dare graze on their grass.

But they don't completely hate me. The smell of cow I ate allures them. They're a vicious group of horned beasts, craving to break their vegan vows.

Back at the table, I'm greeted to a much gentler thing of cows. A platter of the finest of cheeses. Cheese strong. Cheese soft, hard. Cheese with colourful gummy stuff encircling it.

The best is the goat cheese because that population is currently untouched from what the gangster cows spike the earth with.

The sun slinks behind the hills, casting the white stone bricks of the farm in golden rays. These also reflect off the cows, glowing their backs red. One cow pushes another. A signal? Attack while they're possessed by the greatest of cow demons?

The sun falls, leaving the Canadian flag with a few last ray. The cows walk away. Perhaps there's something more vicious that comes out to play.

With the last few golden rays hitting the flag, the dinner guests stand and sing, "O' Canada! ..."

Candles are brought out. The flames dance, splashing yellow against faces. It's story time.

I spook with a journal entry, consisting of my birthday, shadows and a drill. It's okay because the cows are gone.

My poyem, "national symbol," follows. It's the day of the maple leaf and why not read about buck teeth of doom.

Several more stories are told. The Book of Places tells a sad story and a story of a French boy and saying "yes" to everything. A poem is recited from the heart and a letter is read about a gent who captured one. There's also a struggle with a disease that one and many others have stood strong over.

Pie is won for the performance. Delicious crust with fresh berries that grew in these hills and survived the cow taint. *Crème fraîche* to beat.

Clean up and rest up. Going to need it for the next time I run into the cows.

A SIMPLE LIFE
Haley Dagley

This poem is based on a man that Howard told me about when we were first driving from the train station to La Roche d'Hys. This man studied the mandolin at the Paris Conservatory of Music. When his parents passed away, none of his four older brothers wanted to take over the family-run wheat farm because they did not want to move back into the rural area. This man left Paris to take it over, and, according to Howard, he still lives there today.

Sun streams through the only small window in the man's bedroom.
He spent last night, like most nights, in the company of his mandolin
With two glasses of red to warm him in the cool evening.
He gazes lovingly at the instrument in the corner,
Worn down and beaten up from countless nights of use
His fingers moving smoothly over the tattered strings.

If only he could skip the monotony of the day
And return to making melodies which shatter the silence of his nights.
He makes his black coffee and stares out the window
At the white cows in the distance, his primary audience
Except on the days when the neighbours come to purchase wheat.
Sometimes they bring their children, who beg for a song.
He is only too happy to oblige.

Laughing children and the hooting and tweeting of birds as
        accompaniment
Might not be the entire Paris Conservatory of Music orchestra.
But it will do.
He remembers the words of his *professeurs*
"Un talent naturel!" they proclaimed over and over again
Until at last he developed his raw talent.
Ito practiced, refined skill.

He walks outside until he gets to the barn.
He cracks his back and then begins to sort the wheat
Into organized piles until they make sense to him.
Hard Wheat in one pile for Pasta
Soft wheat in another for the soft, warm bread that he enjoys
       each night.
His fingers move smoothly
over each piece to feel their texture.

"There is a big problem keeping the youth in the rural areas"
Is what the estate lawyers had told him
When explaining to him that none of his four older brothers
Would be taking over the family run wheat mill.
"It was your parents' wish that their legacy would live on."
He thinks back to a beautiful girl
With a voice so pure and unrefined

Of course he could never have expected her to leave a glamorous
       life in the city
To marry a man who runs his family's wheat farm.
"What a sacrifice, giving up everything
To keep his family legacy alive!"
They exclaimed, when he returned home with one trunk of clothes
And his beloved Mandolin.
"Sacrifice or fear of failure to reach something that could be
       unattainable?"

That is something that he will ask himself
During every single long, quiet night to come.
This place is perfect for contemplation and self-reflection,
Maybe too perfect.
The day is uneventful, and ends as they usually do
He sits in his chair by the fire

His fingers move slowly over each string of the mandolin
He imagines that her voice is singing along
Building strength as the chords progress
And feels the notes vibrate through him
As they shimmer off into the dark night.

SEE AND THINK.
Priscilla Bernauer

When I see cows and fuschia lipstick
and poppies on the side of the road,
I think of La Roche d'Hys
and my friends
and the way there.
I see power adaptors, crunchtime
deadlines, and the best rabbit I
have had in a while.
This was my first time eating rabbit.
I want to write, and sleep, and read to you.
That drive is in thanks to La Roche d'Hys.
True story. No metaphors.

PEOPLE OF PLACES
Jenna Bontorin

A sign to say we have arrived
Lets heart leap from chest and hope arise
Learning names over the first meal
Jeannette Lisa Haley Asil

A movie screen outside your window
Carving a soul to make it hollow
Hop on the bus with a full suitcase
Get a friendly punch in the face

The White Beauty wandering here and there
Keeps the passing man from care
Moving up and over the hill
Marty Howard Jess and Gill

Reading at the end of the day
Works magic in every way
Music to play and songs to sing
Bird sun sky wings

Hop over cobblestones and shuffle feet
Hands to shake and people to meet
Though not a word of French to say
Ashly Haley Priscilla and Jay

The wine is more than to be drunk
In our chairs we sleepily slunk
Up to bed we contently go
Saying yes maybe probably no

Step down to the market of Dijon
Through kind strangers move along
Buy a hat a scarf or three
Howard narrates all places we see

Can you put Paris in a word or two
Or learn in ten days what you thought you knew
Talk about Callaghan and all his luck
Caitlyn Angelica Carly and Chuck

Hold on tight to the Paris metro
Curving through the belly of the beast
And what then is Burgundy
But a Moveable Feast

DANS LA CITÉ
Caitlyn Gray

I woke up today
Avec la cité
Though, in truth,
The city doesn't sleep
Always a rumble, a cry, a squeal, a wail

La cité
Elle est très différent

From home
And from the hills of Burgundy

There, I woke up with the green
Watched the sun rouse the hills
Shake them gently from their dewy slumber

La cité
Bourgogne
They awaken me in different ways
But each ensures
That I am ready
For the day ahead

STARTING MY DAYS
Jay Rankin

la roche d'hys

When you do something nice for someone, forget it immediately.
When someone does something nice for you, never forget it.

> —advice from Jim Haynes' father to Jim

JULY 1

On the road again
Just can't wait to get on the road again
The life I love making music with my friends
And I can't wait to get on the road again
> —Willie Nelson, "On the Road Again"

JULY 2

Writing had to do with the right relationship between the words
and the thing or person being described: the words should be as
transparent as glass, and every time a writer used a brilliant
phrase to prove himself witty or clever he merely took the mind
of the reader away from the object and directed it to himself; he
became simply a performer.

> —Morley Callaghan

JULY 3

give me my coke

says he
pedal against the floor
blasting through land where wine
cost four and coke
cost more

i want my coke
he presses on
an addict
bloodshot spiderwebs dancing
in the whites

pausing only
for red shutters
and pale bricks

tires crunch into driveway
he reaches for
white swirls
red can
crack
and bubbles
rise into his mouth

JULY 4

Woke up to mists covering the fields of La Roche d'Hys.

JULY 5

People talk of the old man and the sea, but why not the old man and the farm? Or the writers on the farm, painting pictures with words and words with pictures.

JULY 6

Refer to the "Dear Paris," letter.

JULY 7

That hurt a lot!

  —Ashly's response to getting sucker-punched in the face from a man leaving the bus in Paris yesterday, which, when mentioned, makes Jenna bawl out in laughs

journey home

After writing a story I was always empty and both sad and happy, as though I had made love, and I was sure this was a very good story although I would not know truly how good until I read it over the next day.

—Ernest Hemingway

JULY 8

hys swam the nile
deserts
hills
   & forest
stopped
at rolling
burgundian hills

struck rock from mountain
& let flow
its healing waters

JULY 9

brides of burgundy

you all graze along
       growing green hills
leather gowns shining
       white with sol's heat

you wait for *hys*
to rise from his rock

& pronounce you
cows & bull

JULY 10

sky
      meet ocean
ocean
      meet sky
come
      turbulence
      & high seas

DEAR TYLER (JULY 6TH, 2013)
Ashly Flannery

Yesterday we spent the day in Dijon. I wandered the city alone for a good portion of the morning, stopping to photograph interesting doorways and shop fronts. This is the first day of the course that I can actually see what Hemingway and Callaghan were talking about. France is this magical place stuck in a time warp. The old mixed with the new. It must have been amazing in the 20s. Each new doorway seems the beginning of a new and very possible adventure. Moving through the people walking around the market, ducking under scarves, hats and dresses, the smell of cigarettes and coffee. I can see why the lost generation of writers came to France to write. Came to Paris to write. Dijon is like Paris only less crowded and less smelly in the heat. The atmosphere is just different here than anywhere else I've ever been. The busy hustle and bustle of North American life just does not apply here. Art is appreciated and displayed willingly and at random. I am surrounded by the inspirational work of those from this country's rich history, present and future. Food is a celebration not only a step along the refuelling assembly line. Old men sit and talk over espresso for hours. Espresso, you know the coffee that comes in the tiny cups! I can't even believe how amazing the croissants are here. I guess to be fair the French do love their butter.

Funny enough, as I'm walking down the streets taking in what should be the foundation of life, my mind drifts back to the cows. They seem to embody these ideals. Maybe it was thinking about all that butter that did it but here I am photographing the most amazing blue door I have ever seen and all I can think about are the damn cows. Those beautiful Beauties, so calm, collected, don't they know that they will most likely be eaten within the next year? I doubt it. Honestly if they did I doubt that they would change a thing about the way they live their lives. Gracefully gallivanting through the tall grass, they are happy as pigs in shit. I will seriously never get over the feeling of looking into their big brown eyes and being completely at peace with who I am as a person. How often has that happened to you in your life? Ever? "Keep it simple stupid" seems like such a cliché phrase to use right now but it's the only one I have. It started to rain two days ago in the afternoon, I looked out my window and from there I could see the Beauties gently jogging to the overhanging tree to keep from getting wet. It was almost as if they didn't want to ruin their velvet/leather coats yet they were so carefree. They reminded me of children playing in puddles or kids playfully trying to run between the raindrops to keep from getting wet, clumsy, gleeful and simply serene. All feelings I was hoping to develop while on this course but can't seem to get a grasp.

I'm snapped back into the present moment of Dijon by the sound of church bells. I leave my beautiful blue door and make my way towards the sound. Funny how I never really associate church bells with the tolling of time, but that's exactly what they do isn't it? It makes me wonder how Hemingway and Callaghan felt when it came time for writing. Did they think that they were only going to be inspired for so long? Did they think that by staying in a place like Paris, France would slow the passing of time? Just because the French function on a time schedule that is so completely far from our own did they think that this would afford them a certain sense of immortality? Probably. I know it did that for me. As long as I could keep myself in the moment, surrounded by French clichés and cafes I would be able to skirt the realities of time and age.

Being so much older than most of the other students on the course makes me so uncomfortable when it comes to writing. They are so talented and motivated to write and I can't bring myself to express any thought or feeling on paper. I think it might be age that makes you scared. No that's not true, I was even more terrified at their age. I think for Hemingway age was a huge factor in his writing. As time went on he felt like he was becoming less and less relevant in the creative world. New and upcoming writers like Callaghan were pushing him from the limelight, or so he thought. To write you need to live and experience otherwise where does inspiration come from? I think he started to feel as if he was losing his inspiration and therefore losing his talent. His bravado was probably a tactic to distract away from his inadequacies as a personable man. When I think about him as a person I feel bad for him, when I think of him as a writer I hate him. I'm jealous of his skill and success. I will never be a Hemingway but maybe one day I will be a Flannery.

I find my way to the source of my time passing; a grand church at the end of the market surrounded in gargoyles. I love gargoyles. They remind me completely of a time long past. I don't linger long as I don't want to be reminded of my time. I photograph the stone beasts and move on. The whole time the camera is to my eye I'm trying to remember everything we learned two days ago from a photographer we met. He didn't pick up a camera until he was in his early twenties and from there didn't actually begin his career as a photographer until his late twenties. Maybe there is still hope for me. Fuck, I hope so. I bumped into Jay shortly before the church so we're now wandering the streets together. We're following this weird trail of owls on the ground. We're idiots; the owl is the representative bird of Dijon. The trail was set up to lead visitors to landmarks around the city; it's a tourism ploy. It half worked. We have no idea where we are going or what we are doing and the owls provide us with a game. Needless to say, I fill a memory card of photos and so does Jay.

It was a really long day and I was happy when it came to an end. Dijon was my escape into the 20s and the minds of Hemingway and Callaghan. I never want to forget the feeling of inspiration from a coloured door or the amusement of wandering an afternoon away following a path of owls. I felt a creative license to do whatever I wanted whenever I wanted purely to express myself. I think this was the first night I really read something aloud to the group. I was terrified and guarded and for the first time I understood where Hemingway was coming from. I hated him less after that night.

EUROPEAN BROWNIES
Angelica Lachance

I looked into the display case, and there were two cameras propped up under the glass. This shouldn't have come as any sort of a surprise to me; it was a photography museum after all. But the lens looked like it was attached to the rest of the camera with a miniature red accordion. Luckily for me, my professor, also a photographer and well beyond my years, was right next to me.

"Hey Marty, do you know what these are?"

"Oh! Those are brownies! I used to have one of those lying around my house when I was younger."

"Brownies?" I said as my stomach began to rumble. It seemed that I had picked the wrong day to miss breakfast. "I could go for one of those right now."

Joking aside, he began to describe how they worked to me. I was fascinated by how you could take a picture while the camera was just above your waist because of the placement of the viewfinder. I loved the mini-history lesson and I thought they looked really neat, but I moved on without thinking too much about them, even though the rumbling in my stomach did not subside.

*　*　*　*　*　*

A few days later, I was browsing a market in the streets of Dijon, France. I was glancing through antiques, when suddenly I saw a small shape that looked like it had the folds of an accordion protruding out of it. It looked all too familiar, and it only took me a moment to see that it was the same model of brownie that I had questioned just a couple of days before. It wore its age well, but I picked it up in fear wondering if I could even afford to touch it. I turned it over and saw the price sticker that read "8 euro." I was filled with excitement, and I quickly pulled out and handed over the money to the camera's owner. I had never seen anything like this in my life, outside of the two in the museum casing, and there was no way to know when I would stumble upon one again. I excitedly put it in my bag, anxious to show the others I was travelling with what I had found.

* * * * * *

When we returned to our French countryside house, I headed inside towards my professor who was sitting in a chair by the window.

"Do you want to see what I bought? I think you're really going to like it."

I pulled out a chair, pulled out the case, and finally pulled out the camera and handed it to him.

"Wow! Where did you find this?!"

I explained the Dijon market and how I had stumbled upon the very same camera I had inquired about just days before, but nothing could have prepared me for his response.

"Congratulations! I'm so happy for you!"

Of all the reactions I expected, congratulating me on my find was never something that I considered. I was almost confused by him saying this. As he continued to share in my excitement and show the others what I had found, I found myself fighting back tears. There I was, sharing my passion for history and photography with someone who really understood it too. I could see his love for its history and its purpose in the way that he handled it as gently as a child, and I felt that I was experiencing something that I wouldn't forget.

* * * * * *

The camera now sits on a shelf, bearing its witness to history and its ability to withstand the forces of aging and time. When I see it, it reminds me of my curiosity in the photography museum I first saw one at in the north of France. It reminds me of my passion for photography and gives me an appreciation for the advances in technology since its day. It reminds me of my second European adventure and the antique markets that bear witness to history. It fills me with wonder about the places it has seen and the moments it has captured. And now, it also reminds me of that moment in the front room in the house in France where that camera became one of my most prized possessions.

MY EXPERIENCE
Priscilla Bernauer

"What does 'what if?' mean to you?"

When you have no time for dead men, lifelong choices, or feminism, I prescribe a slice of Époisses.

I prefer hard cheese myself, but as you chew this, your legs become longer and each step is a hundred kilometres.

Take thirty steps and you have Gillian, the girl who says yes in a good way. You have Jeanette, who makes you mean it when you clap.

You have Howard, who wants you to see the world he sees. He finds complete happiness when you find your own world in the lavender stocks.

When you hide behind metaphor for fear people will know you actually said something, peek your head out the window as Caitlyn and Ashly escape a stampede of cows.

Watch a girl peek her head out of the same window waiting for France to rain. It is the first rain she has ever seen.

Listen to Carly and Lisa discuss family values.

If you are in a hurry to know your life is going nowhere, watch the man who sells you wine make his cat move like an accordion.

Comfort a nauseated Haley as the world changes its axis in front of her eyes.

Go to a church. Stand in awe when someone says, "this is older than the English language."

Try to quote a Shakespearean play you have known completely for ten years. Realize it has been replaced by hundreds of images your camera could not save.

Lisa sits beside me as we look at hills roll in the wind like refugee canary diamonds. "I can see a poem forming in your head" she says.

You know what? I think so.

A POSTCARD FROM PARIS
Carly Butler

Before I left Windsor in January of 2013, Marty extended an invitation for me to join his writing group in France as a speaker. Being in the "Yes" mindset made for an easy decision on my part. "Of course I'll be there. I would love to join you," slipped out of mouth without a thought.

This was days before departing on a 6-month journey retracing the steps of my British war bride Grandmother outlined in 110 love letters that she penned to my Grandfather 67 years earlier. They were dated January to July of 1946.

Marty's advice to me was simple: write every day about what you see, what you hear, and what you feel. And that is what I did.

As I booked the Eurorail train from London to Paris, I made a call home to see if my mother had any photographs of my Grandmother in Paris. This scanned image is what showed up in my inbox. Another moment in time to recreate, years later. It's almost as if the path was being created for me before my own eyes.

As we pulled up to the farm, my only plan was to connect and engage with the beautiful students who had come all this way. To share my story and what I had learned. Little did I know that the summer nights spent under the stars sharing a meal of beef bourguignon that lasted for hours drinking French wine and decadent cheese in some of the richest conversations I had ever had, would forever change me. And it all seemed to boil down to this: we all have a story. And life stories need to be honoured, held in the hands of those who are worthy. Life stories are beautifully raw, and heartbreakingly gorgeous. And when living those lives wholeheartedly and honouring the path that's being created for you, that is when you're living a life aligned with your dreams.

June 30th, 2013

Dear Grama,

Just a quick postcard to tell you what a lovely time I've been having in the enchanting city of Paris. I've spent time wandering the book & art stalls along the Seine stealing glances at Notre Dame in between. I've spent an afternoon at cafes with colourful canopies & outward facing seats so the patrons can watch the world go by. I've wandered uphill to Montmartre taking in the picturesque rod-iron terraces lined with wooden shutters & flower boxes. The historical beauty of Paris is incredible and I've been officially swept off my feet by the love & romance that radiates from this city.

I was also sure to visit the one and only Eiffel Tower—it literally made me jump up & down with excitement when it came into sight. As we climbed up to get the best view of the breathtaking structure, I once again lined myself up to the exact place that you stood many years before. I thought of the beauty of that moment. This was at a time that you & Papa had been reunited for many years, it was a trip you two did with a group of war-brides that you travelled the world with, and it was just a teeny, tiny glimpse of your happily every after.

It fills me with love, hope & gratitude.

With a granddaughter's love & admiration,

Carly xoxo

MERCI, BURGUNDY
Lisa Salfi

I met you first at the bank.
I, likely tired, bearing black,
headed to another night of
slinging drinks, projectile vomit,
and drunken dialogue at Papa C's.

I didn't notice you.
Too self-involved and foggy—
unsure about life and
suffering paralysis by status quo.

We probably shared pleasant small chat,
both young women in the industry of
customer service.
You deposited money into my account,
and nothing into my memory.

We met once again at Gare Bercy.
4000 miles away from mundanity,
you told me what I did not know
and did not ask
at the bank that day.
With a smile and a rare sparkle in your eye,
you told me of inspiration and courage.
You told me of following dreams.

You told me of publicity,
BBC breakfast, internet interviews.
You told me of family and legacy.
You told me of success.
You told me of choice.

And, like the bright rays of Being
over the lush green hills of La Roche d'Hys,
the light of your journey
burned through my fog.

We became friends.
We chat about food and flatulence
and boys and lipstick and life.
We talk about fear.

You're still scared, still unsure,
still concerned of others' perception
of what you are doing, what you will do.
You're afraid to admit the revelation
that all you really want is a simple life.

I am afraid I will never have your courage.
Your confident yet humble attitude.
That sparkle.

Looking out to the bright, azure summer sky,
The White Beauties,
The multiple shades of green,
And this magical, rolling, Burgundian landscape,
I am forced to remember that life is a gift.

Recalling the history of La Roche d'Hys,
I know that this gift may be
returned to its Creator
in the smallest fraction of time.

And I wonder—
Will I act?
Will I have courage?
Will I follow my dreams?
What will I do next?

I really met you here.
Merci, Burgundy.

FRANCE REFLECTIONS
Asil Moussa

July 3, 2013 — "Pastry Shop"

Today at a pastry shop in France, I wanted to buy what I thought looked like a pizza pastry. The woman looked at me and then tried her very best to explain in French that the "pizza" had ham in it. With the help of a friend, I understood what she was saying. I could not believe how much strangers look out for you here. She realized I was Muslim, knew I didn't eat pork, and cared enough to tell me, even though she didn't have to and despite the language barrier. Needless to say, I went back to her shop 3 times that afternoon for chocolate croissants... and I brought more friends.

July 5, 2013 — "The Visitor"

During an indoor conversation about literature, the bird in the room started haphazardly flying and the two cats leaped onto the bookshelf and chair with piercing stares at the wall. We looked round and realized what had caused the commotion: this long, slim snake was slithering out of an opening in the wall. And to think I was scared of the tiny spider that was climbing my camera five seconds ago.

July 8, 2013 — "The Lesson"

This is my last night at La Roche d'Hys in Burgundy, France. I cannot even begin to describe how incredible this experience has been. It taught me so many things about the world, people, writing, art, and myself.

But above all, it taught me to have Courage. The courage to share thoughts, stories, poetry, and read out loud. The courage to travel more, adventure, and explore. The courage to write no matter how good or bad it is at first. The courage to love, laugh and cry, have deep conversations, and connect with strangers who I know have touched my heart forever. The courage to live in the moment and be fully present. The courage to seek knowledge and learn wholeheartedly everyday. The courage to be silly and have fun. The courage to follow my dreams, do what I love, and live the life I wish to live. And most of all, the courage to believe in myself.

Thank you, La Roche d'Hys. Thank you, France. And most importantly, thank you to all the beautiful people I have met on this extraordinary journey. You have inspired me in more ways than I can count, and I hope we meet again. *Merci.*

FORGET GEOGRAPHY
Lisa Salfi

*That was called transplanting yourself, I thought, and it could be
as necessary with people as with other sorts of growing things.*

—Ernest Hemingway, *A Moveable Feast*

Forget geography.

I need to transplant myself from my skin.
Shed from my constrictive surroundings
like the curious snake at Sheila's country house.
Slip it off quietly and graciously before
it explodes all around me,
making a mess out of chaos.
Leave it hanging, limp and transparent,
over the rocky edge on which I
now balance.
Replant my roots in healthier soil.
Aerated soil that lets me breathe and grow
and bask in the sunlight of a new day,
a new me.

OUR LAST DAY
Priscilla Bernauer

On the last day with our white cows,
Howard invited us for a swim.
The gravel was coarser than
sand and I ran into the lake
to tread water. The adults
sunbathed on the beach while I
played with the gravel.

"You finally left that camera
at home. That's good. Enjoy
this view!"

HILLS & MEMORIES
Caitlyn Gray

Sitting before the hills is a bloody kind of beautiful
It was not so long ago that I myself had some marvellous hills
close to home

But time flies when in one hand you've got classes and in another
jobs and in another family and in another friends and in another
your past and in another your future and then somehow in your
present you stumble and pause for just a moment
And wonder
What mutation caused you to grow so many hands in the first place
And maybe you need a little surgery
But at the very least
You need a little change

I believe in healing waters the way I believe in fairies
The way fiction is, somewhere, a truth
I'll keep peering into woodlands
I'll keep dipping in my fingers
Because maybe by now
Somewhere has become Here

I do believe that the past is not to be escaped
Should not be escaped
Hold your memories close
They are before you, to be touched and loved and experienced again
But tweaked in the most bloody and beautiful way

I close my eyes against the hills
Just a moment, paused
Because they remind of me of Old Home
My heart
Dripping blood, and it hurts
Pumping blood because I'm alive
And ready
For new beginnings
And all that the hills have to give

ONE DAY
Gillian Cott

On a single day, Germans visit a farm in a small rural village in Burgundy. They impose themselves on the woman of the house. They drink the family's wine, eat their rationed bread. They have heard that the resistance movement is growing so they inspect the farm. Guns are found in the ceiling of the bread oven.

On a day in 1944, the man who lived on the farm is brought to the bottom of a hill and killed for resisting German occupation. On the same day, the farm is burned to the ground. The smoke is so thick it could choke a man. The bright white clouds, normally absent of any colour, and the deep blue sky aren't visible from behind the black smog. For the widow, every day is spent missing his presence, his smile, the way he whispered, "Je t'aime" into her ear as he passed her in the hall.

On another day, not long after, villagers of the same small rural village in Burgundy capture three German soldiers and ask the same widow what to do with the prisoners. On that day, her decision is guided by revenge. Kill them.

In a day, people go to the cinema or the market. There is nothing remarkable about these days, though perhaps the sky looked exceptionally blue and crisp, or you saw peonies begin to bloom in the springtime as you smelled lilac and magnolias in the sugary air. One day, sixty years later, a woman will find letters written between lovers during World War II. These lovers will end up being her grandparents. The granddaughter will choose to follow the steps of her grandmother, a war bride living in England. She will move abroad, and will go to the cinema and the market. She will share her stories with strangers, women in bold lipstick, plump men, curious students. Then she will write a book about adventure, love, and letter-writing.

On a Sunday, every week, a man has a dinner party in Paris. 110 people show up. The people who come don't sit down in his small atelier, tiled black and white and decorated in books, but they eat well, have good conversations, and may meet a Lulu from Chicago.

On a day you happen to take a drive to Grosbois Reservoir, you watch a child take her first steps. She fumbles in her little sandals and eventually falls on tiny sand-coloured pebbles, but this is the start of her big journey. And one day, maybe she will live in France, run a 100 kilometer marathon, or write a book about her adventure.

Over ten days, students visiting a rebuilt farm in rural Burgundy are inspired by stories of the German occupation, of grandparents' letters, of Paris parties. They share poetry with you and you are moved. You tell them you love them and you mean it because you are learning, every day, that life is about other people. It's about big dinners, conversations so long they must be continued the following morning, stars shining on smiling faces, and memories that leave you tied together like the stems of roses leaning into the stone warmth of the farm we shared.

In a day, if you listen with patience, you will hear the sound of people's hearts beating in time with the stories they choose to share. You will be told about hitchhiking across Canada with only a five-dollar bill, of getting locked out of apartments in Italy, of libraries in Egypt, of dead sisters, and of a healing spring near an escarpment that has made people feel small since the pagans believed in Isis. You will hear poetry in people's simple sentences and you will cry when poems are written and recited because life, her challenges and coincidences, the colour of the sky at sunset, the sound of cows mooing in the morning, the taste of cheese, and the fact that flowers bloom every spring, seem too perfect to be written about. If you look closely, you will see moths' wings move lavender flowers in the sun and you will realize that you are just like them, small but strong, with a heartbeat like butterfly wings.

WHAT CAN I LEARN FROM JIM? PAST AND PRESENT
Haley Dagley

Out of all of the incredibly interesting people that we met in France, there was one person who I know will stick with me for my entire life. Jim Haynes is a man who does not live up to society's standards of what is normal, or how we should treat one another. In my opinion, this is a good thing. Spending an hour or two in Jim's home made more of an impression on me then I ever would have thought possible. It struck me that there are some things that I, along with most other people living on this earth for that matter, can learn from him.

After completing a couple of years of post-secondary school, Jim Haynes received a letter requesting that he serve in the American Military. As he was walking home one day, he saw a poster for the American Air Force. He enlisted in the air force, and in two weeks' time he found himself heading off for training camp. Once he had arrived at training camp, he decided to take his fate into his own hands. He tracked down the lieutenant who was going to be deciding where he would end up and asked where he was going to be stationed. The lieutenant told him that he could be stationed anywhere in the world and asked him where he would like to go, so he requested the smallest military base in Eastern Europe. It was then that he found himself in Edinburgh.

This, right here, is a clear demonstration of the first thing that we should learn from Jim. Sometimes in life, you need to take a chance and ask for what you want. All too often, people are fully aware that they are not getting what they need out of life or from another person but they are too afraid to speak up about it. One hour with Jim was enough to determine that there is nothing in this world that he would be afraid to ask of someone, but this goes both ways. There is also nothing in the world that he would be afraid to offer to someone.

When Jim got to Edinburgh, he was quick to request something else that he really wanted. He asked his lieutenant if it would be possible for him to live off of the army base. When asked why, he said that he wished to attend the local university during the day and he would work his post by night. His lieutenant agreed to this, which is another testament to the power of asking for what you want. After serving with the air force while attending university for a couple of years, Jim requested an early discharge. Once again his wish was granted.

He decided to stay in Edinburgh for school, a decision that his parents did not agree with. He stayed anyways, which meant that his parents were no longer paying for his living expenses. Because of this, he decided to buy and run a paperback bookshop. All he needed was a location, which he found one day when he walked past an old antique store. He went inside and asked the woman working there if she would sell the shop to him, and she said that she was getting old and should probably retire so she would sell it to him for today's equivalent of 600 pounds. This is the next thing that we can learn from Jim. Sometimes in life, you need to go for the things that you want despite the opinions of others who might not agree with what you are doing. If Jim had listened to his parents and left Edinburgh, his life would have been very different. Fortunately, he knew from a young age how to go after the things that he wanted in order to turn his dreams into a reality.

Over the years, Jim would accomplish way too many notable things to list. Through it all, the biggest accomplishment that he would make would be the impact that he would have on the countless lives of the people around him. One thing about Jim is that to him, every single person on this earth is equal. While this is something that many people say, in Jim's case I truly believe that he means it. He could he hanging out with a student like me or a celebrity, and I honestly believe that he would treat us both the exact same. That is something else that we can learn from Jim. Everyone is important. Period.

To this very day, there are two things that are absolute constants in Jim's life. The first is that he regularly takes people into his home, whether it is for a couple of weeks, a month, or a year. Whether he knows these people well or not, if they want to stay in Paris, Jim finds joy and happiness out of helping them out by giving them a place to stay. The second is that he hosts elaborate dinner parties every Sunday night. People from all over the world and all different walks of life come out to these dinner parties, and I can only imagine that attending one would be the opportunity of a lifetime.

This is the final and perhaps the most important thing that we can learn from Jim. Never be afraid to give all of yourself to the people that you meet. Everyone has something to offer, and we should never be afraid to put ourselves out there to people and to take what they have in return. This was made clear when a random woman from Chicago named Lulu phoned Jim in the middle of our conversation with him. He had never met her or even heard of her before, but she was calling to ask him if she could attend his dinner party the following night. Jim had already told us earlier that he had over 100 people coming the next night, and that his maximum capacity was generally 100. Even still, Jim did not even hesitate to tell the woman that she was more than welcome. Once he hung up, he told us jokingly that he can never turn down a woman named Lulu.

As we were leaving, all of us were eager to purchase Jim's biography. When someone inquired about the price, Jim was quick to tell them that his policy is to charge each person what they can afford. This is a pretty clear summary of the type of person that Jim is. As he autographed our copies one by one, he was sure to include a unique comment in each person's book. As I sat next to him while he autographed mine, I was eager to see what he would write. When we left his house, I opened up the front cover and read the cursive and a smile formed on my face. "Haley, are you a comet?" A comet is something that races across a typical black night sky, turning it into something new, different, and exhilarating. It is something that most people only have the chance to see once in a lifetime. I am not sure whether I am a comet or not, but one thing is for certain: Jim fits that description perfectly, as I have never met anyone like him in my life and do not think that I ever will again.

DEAR PARIS
Jay Rankin

I feel sorry for you—you share a name with that love-struck insensitive jerk that fucked over Troy. Your cobblestone streets beat the sun's golden rays 'gainst my skin while the flowing Seine bends them towards my eyes. Your gypsies love to dance and itch their fingers towards my pockets, while waiters refuse *mon vert d'eau* and salt my tongue with overpriced-burnt café.

& back in burgundy, priscilla tells me that she loves "cheating" & laughs when i tell her this. and beaten tongues whip word, lashing at the education system & that forbidden topic known as bullying. & jenna claims that she's "into girls now." & we laugh because why not—& we're just joking

& with a pass of the rosé & a splash of *pamplemousse* we're back with the most interesting man in the world. pull a jim haynes & say yes to everything. say yes to his extravagant sunday night parties. & it's okay because there's francesco, the swimming-cooking-*pianiste*-architect who someone said was the guy version of jenna & gillian has the hots for. & say yes to cooking for jim because it's close to jay &—

there was a cow grazing at the grass, pale head poking through the fence, reaching to join our conversation. & this time my foot did not catch the stone wall to sway me to french kiss *la terre*

& i wish a good dinner to all my favourite hippies

sincerely, shoving that cup down *la poubelle*,

j

THE PARIS SUBWAY EXPERIENCE
Asil Moussa

The subways of Paris have a life of their own. When a group of us chose this method of transportation, I didn't think anything of it. I didn't think that it was going to be particularly dangerous, life-threatening, or uncomfortable. But I was wrong. On so many levels. You see, we forgot one important detail in our calculation to ride the subway: it was lunch hour. And that changes everything. Let me explain: everyone in France goes home during lunch hour. It's like rush hour on crack. Just to get on the subway is a fight to the death. People are shoving and pushing and elbowing you in the face!

But the challenge begins even before that. First we spent 10 whole minutes staring at the subway map and asking every English-speaking stranger in the vicinity the directions to get to the Latin district via subway. And then we spent another 20 minutes finding our way to three other subway stations because, apparently, the one we needed to go on was under construction and the others don't have the metro we needed. Finally at our desired station, we spent another five minutes looking at the map and asking strangers for directions and confirming what they've told us. After we knew that this is where we needed to be, we simply inserted our ticket to go through. But nothing is ever that simple on the Paris subway. No, I forgot to mention that 40% of the time, our old ticket didn't work and we had to stand in line for another 10 minutes to get a new one. And then it was finally time to frantically look for our metro, climbing up and down multiple cases of stairs in search for it. And alas, we found it, but in front of it and all around us, stood our opponents: about 100 people who needed to get on the same metro. This was the battleground. And it was hot as hell. I immediately started sweating and getting fidgety. After what seemed like forever, the much-anticipated subway arrived and the doors opened. Chaos erupted. People tried to squeeze their way out of the subway while others were pushing themselves in. The weak were left behind to await the next metro and fight the battle again. I hoped for the miracle that my entire group of friends would manage to get on the metro; sometimes it happens and this time, it did.

Inside the subway was a whole different level of hell. I didn't even know that humans could survive that high a temperature. The nastiest thing in the world is having people's sweat on your own body and that's what happened today. That's how closely pressed together everyone was. Ew! You could literally see the sweat beads on men's beards and make-up melting off women's faces, as their scorching arms touched yours. Some people, including myself, still found it necessary to weasel their arms through the entangled mass of bodies and purses to hold onto one of the metal poles, because no matter how close we were to each other, there was still the possibility that the subway might lurch and send my head into someone's tooth. And I did not want that to happen.

As I held my massive camera close and pointed it down, I mentally scolded myself for not putted it in my purse before we got on the subway. Its hard, plastic body jammed into my ribs. I had thankfully put the lens cap on before though, so I didn't have to worry about any lens scratches.

I stood as straight as I could and hoped my stop would come fast. As I waited, an array of smells made their way through my nose, and I could barely breathe over the fumes of suffocating sweat, overpowering cologne, cheap perfume, and sickly sweet vanilla body spray. Everyone was breathing in everyone's air. It was all carbon monoxide. I thought how if some of us fainted due to the lack of oxygen, we'd never notice because the bodies would probably keep standing up straight due to the lack of room to even shift slightly, let alone fall.

As I stood there, sweating off half my weight, I noticed that the man two people away from me, who was talking on the phone through Bluetooth, was speaking in Arabic. It was clearly audible because everyone else was talking quietly or in whispers, whereas this guy was talking at a normal level. I wondered how he could bring himself to talk under the current circumstances of the front of his body being pressed against another's side. Maybe he was used to it, I thought, used to having no room to even tap his cell phone to end the conversation. For lack of better things to do, I listened to what he was saying, trying to figure out what could be so important that he had to hog all the oxygen on the metro talking about it. His Arabic wasn't a dialect that I clearly understood so I shrugged it off and blocked out all the little words here and there that I caught.

After a couple of minutes, the subway cleared nearly a third of its people and now there was actually room to breathe. But not that much. The man turned towards me. I looked away. When I turned back in his direction a few seconds later, he was still looking at me. Tall, tanned, and bald, he could easily be 30 years old. Though I wouldn't be surprised if he was 40. He nodded at me to get my attention. "You speak Arabic?" he said in Arabic. "Yes." I replied. The rest of our conversation was in Arabic, but I'll write it here in English.

"Where are you from?" he asked me.

I could barely understand what he was saying. "Canada," I replied.

"I know," he glanced over at my friends, who had spoken English earlier. "I mean originally, where are you from?"

Oh, I should've known. It was the first question all Arabs ask each other. "Egypt," I answered.

He smiled. "What neighbourhood?" he asked.

Yeah. Because that's not creepy at all. I told him the neighbourhood.

"Oh!" he grinned. "Everything I know, I know from the movies," he said in an Egyptian dialect.

I smiled. Most Arabs I meet often tell me that they know Egyptian from watching a lot of Arabic films and TV, and since the Arab world's Hollywood is in Egypt, that's not hard to believe.

He told me he was from Algeria. That explains the dialect I couldn't understand. He spoke to me now in a pure Egyptian accent, something that he learned from the movies.

Then he went on to ask what I'm studying and what I'm doing in France. He hoped I liked Paris. As we spoke, I could tell people were looking at us, and probably wondering who could carry a conversation in this level of heat.

When he asked how long I was in France, I said 10 days; that's how long my creative writing course in Burgundy was. I think something about how I replied confused him because then he asked if I was married or have kids. I looked at him. "I'm twenty," I said, with a hesitant laugh, "I have neither." After that I stopped talking and I looked down. I wasn't sure whether to be creeped out by his question or just classify it as "Questions Strangers Ask on Subways."

Before he got off at his stop, he said, "Well have a great time in Paris. Happy Ramadan. Peace."

"Thanks. And you, too. Peace," I replied.

And that was my encounter with the Algerian French man on the subway. I love talking to people but I should add that it's super awkward to have a conversation on the metro, because 1: It's freaking hot as hell and you're probably sweating buckets. 2: I feel like everyone can hear what you're saying on the subway. I mean, I guess it's more private when people don't understand the language you're speaking in. But it's still very awkward.

The rest of the subway ride was boring and the humidity was so bad that every time people got up, you could hear the collective sound of their bodies peeling off the hot seats. But despite all the grossness, my tired body persuaded me to sit-down at the finally-free-already-butt-imprinted seat. Through the large metro windows, I watched people stand impatiently as they awaited their subways and their uncomfortable metro-riding fate.

After five long, smelly minutes, we finally arrived at our stop. I could not even describe to you the joy I felt as I climbed the dark underground steps and saw the sunlight.

ABOUT WRITING
Jay Rankin

You see. The problem is that people worry too much. And this worry can inhibit some people from doing what they really want to do—and that can really dampen some great opportunities to write.

To write, somebody needs something to write about. To have that something, they (he/she, whomever) needs to experience something. And to experience something, it requires getting off the buttox and getting out there. And Paris, you have something.

That's why Hemingway left North America. He went to you to soak in your culture and to partake in the writing life there. And yes, he did suffer. For a while he scrounged through pennies and would let himself starve while out working, only so he could crawl home on your streets and eat cheaply. This also led him to discover how hunger honed his senses and made him more observant. And observing is essential to his craft

And that's sort of what I did. I went on a trip that I could hardly afford, just for an experience. Sure, I may not be able to get the newest iPad, get McDonald's everyday or cough up dough for one of those new video-gaming systems coming out, but what I do have is an experience. And this will carry with me until the end of my time (whereas electronics usually last around three years). And the experience will affect every inch of my creative work, which hopefully will last past my time.

And it makes me pretty darn happy—isn't that what life's about?

Creative writing is about communicating images, stories, emotions through words. And sometimes the only way to find these is to go out and find these little trinkets.

And of course, making it interesting. If you've been experiencing the same drab thing day after day, chances are that you don't find it interesting—so why would you write about that?

So. Stop wishing you were a writer. Get out there and be one.

& the eyes of prof, readers, would-be critics stare down students to write, write, write

& it's great to think that nobody's a better writer than another, that we're all the same in this socialist writing class. & that's why France doesn't teach creative writing in university because they think it's useless & not fitting to the fairness of utilitarianism

but it's not the same because everyone needs to read good literature & it's better to read one or two pieces that move you instead of 50 that do nothing & eat the sands of your hourglass. & we're all competitive in the capitalization of pen to paper 'cause that's what pushes us to be better & better & better

& that's why writers bond. because together we can make a dozen. a hundred. untold fathoms of great literature. like waves, scrambling over each other

And Paris, this is why everyone must see you. So. Please write back.

AU REVOIR! — *The label for the bottle Howard cracked open for us to celebrate our last night at the farm.*